The PRESS Series:
Book One

"It's Okay to Cry"

By Altovise Pelzer

Unless otherwise indicated, all scripture quotations are taken from the New Living Translation (NLT) version of the Bible

It's Okay to Cry

Table of Contents

Introduction

Some people advocate that living life is the best teacher. That is true if you are stubborn, prideful or ignorant to the people who God has placed in your life. C.S. Lewis said, "Experience: that most brutal of teachers. But you learn, my God do you learn."

I have found that you can learn just as much from someone else's situations as you do from your own. Now don't be mistaken. There are some things we must go through in order to gain understanding and wisdom but I'm referring to the situations that we endured because of our own choices. We have been given the blueprint of life, through history in the natural as well as the spiritual, for us to sift through and pull apart. If you have troubles that seem bigger than you just read about David. Think that God can't use you then read about Moses or Saul. The good, the bad and the ugly are all laid out for you to read and apply to your own situations.

For those who need something a little more up to date we look at the testimony and lives of others. Through books, video and old fashion talking we can be educated and trained. It is evident that there is more than one road to your destiny. Some choose the hard road, embracing difficulties with the tenacity to win, and others choose the easier road, unwilling to fight for what God has said was yours. Understand that there is no such thing as an easy road. The difference is in the journey which is determined by the decisions we make everyday. Truthfully it's your decisions that have brought you to this point in your life through your actions and reactions. Just as it takes only one wrong turn to get lost it takes one decision to move from faith to fear. Let's be honest, not every decision we make is a good one when left to our own devices. Don't get discouraged because it only takes one action to get you back on track.

In "The PRESS Series" I hope to give you a personal view of how your decisions can be bright in Christ or dim in self. My prayer is that you will be able to eat the meat and throw out the fat when it comes to your own tough times. In Mark 4, there is the picture of what it means to go through tough situations. Here are the disciples, doing what Jesus told them to do. They are "going to the other side". Then a storm comes. I can almost imagine the boat rocking back and forth sending the disciples sliding and falling across the boat. I'm quite sure a few must have fallen during that storm. I am sure that those who fell got back up. Whether it was during the storm with help from something stable or after Jesus calmed the waves. We know that they all got back up because they all made it off the boat. The situations that knock us on our rear ends usually become determining factors to our success as well as the success of others. A fork in the road can lead us to self-pity or self-worth. Which road do you travel?

February of 2009 it was discovered that my two young daughters were being molested by their stepbrother. My husband and I had separated two years prior and they would go to visit him on the weekends. As a single mother, I made it a habit of asking my children how their day went or how their weekend went. The answer I received this time wasn't one I was ready for. Who knew that this Sunday would be different? Who knew the effect that day would have on my children and me? God knew it! I just wasn't at the point where I really knew Him.

The news was a blow to my family and my pride. As a parent we hope to be able to shield our children from everything. How could I let this happen? I didn't physically allow it to happen, but that did notstop the question from popping in my head. That's how the enemy attacks us. He will make it seem like we did something wrong but that is not always the case. Even when we are the ones who made a mistake, we are not doomed to burn for all eternity. The effects of this event were devastating both emotionally and mentally. My children suffered terribly because they were no longer allowed to go to their father's home. I truly felt alone dealing with my children being angry all the time, having nightmares, traveling back and forth to court and counseling sessions. That was the point when my heart broke. I would lay awake at night crying and asking God, "Lord, why me?"

During what felt like my darkest moment, my eyes couldn't adjust to see that God's angels were watching over us. That He had placed favor all around us. The young man pleaded guilty so my daughters did not have to come to court. A good girlfriend of mine who had graduated from law school came with me to court and she was able to better explain all of the legal jargon being discussed. My children and I came out stronger because of what we went through. Even now, as I look back at the whole situation I see that there are so many lessons God taught me. Those lessons I plan to share with you in this book. I pray that my experience can help strengthen, push, pull or guide you through a moment that is so dark you can't see where you're going. Know that your latter will be greater and there is always a lesson to be learned.

"Casting all your cares upon him, for he careth for you." I Peter 5:7

I know you must be wondering, "How can I see any lesson when my lights are off or what lesson could be taught after the scars of abuse or rape has you curled up in a fetal position?" One lesson everyone learns after they come out of a situation is that you are stronger than you thought. Think of it as a huge maze. Some sat down and cried in a corner as they rocked to and fro afraid to move out of the corner of fear. Others turned around and went back out the way they came retreating before the fight began. You on the other hand, made it out the other side. You may have some bruises and bumps but you made it. I think about the man in Mark 5. What if the disciples had turned around after the storm in Mark 4? The man that was possessed in Mark 5 would have never received his deliverance and freedom from the bondage he was in. Yes people are still in bondage today. There are still those who cut themselves physically and verbally. Now what will you do when you come out of your maze? Forge onward to the next task orhelp someone?

The maze for you may be addiction, abuse, teen pregnancy, fear, doubt or any number of other things people are fighting with day after day. Every person has gone through a maze at some point in their life and you can see it in how they live today. What started out as a painful crutch has blossomed into a tool for someone else's success. The Lord has brought me a mighty long way but I had to take the necessary steps on my own. A breakthrough is coming, will you stand and wait for it to show up or will you walk towards your destiny.

Altovise C. Pelzer

It's okay to **CRY**!

Cry Scream, Shout and Release.

As a child, when you got hurt you cried. That's simple right? Male, female, cat or dog pain is pain. It could be the pain from falling off a bike or the pain of losing a friend. Somehow, as we grow older we are conditioned by societal beliefs that crying means weakness. We guard ourselves from what others might say or think by putting on a different face.

When my six year old explained to me the details of being molested all I could do was CRY. CRY because my daughter's innocence was now gone, CRY because I couldn't protect my little princess and CRY because the effects of the offense would last longer than her childhood. The day turned from bad to worse when I found out that not one but both of my daughters had been molested. I felt like someone had given me a punch to my chest that left me breathless. Now you know, emotions have a way of running ahead of your mind when you are sad or angry.

I tried to stay calm and be rational. I tried to see things from another viewpoint but at the moment I couldn't see anything through the tears. In the end I was listening to the dial tone, my family was in emotional shambles and I was left with my heart and mind full of questions. Oh, the questions I had. Each question brought a new flow of tears. Imagine having to tell a story over and over again. I felt horrible as a parent making my girls repeat the events that led up to that day to me, the police, doctors, nurses, the lawyer, the therapist and the special victims unit.

The words I that flowed like lava did absolutely nothing to help my situation. During my time of sorrow I had allowed my emotions to take control. Here lies mistake #1. When emotions run free then you have walked out of faith and into fear. Not only was I walking in fear, I was showing my children how to walk in fear. It took me some time to realize that I couldn't have a pity party every time my world was shaken up by circumstances and hardships. Those same circumstances, whether I was victorious over the situation or not, made a difference in my life. The experience gave me the opportunity to become stronger by understanding my strengths and being able to identify my weaknesses. Mistake #2 was the effect of my first mistake. I turned a bad situation worse because of my mouth. An aunt of mine once told me that the Shut Up Ministry is a ministry everyone should be apart of and she was right. Sometimes silence is the best line of defense. I'm referring to silence in the midst of emotional moments. During those times when your emotions are boiling over and you find yourself ready to fight.

"....weeping may endure for a night, but joy cometh in the morning."

Psalm 30:5

When I couldn't see the end of my sorrow God already had a plan in place. At times, we lose heart when we think that Psalms 30:5 is talking about the next day. Nope! It says morning not the next day. When we are in the midst of a situation this dark cloud covers our head where ever we go. People ask us something and we bark and growl. Everything irritates us. That is our own personal night. Here is the point when you need to turn into a flower. Huh? A Flower? Yes a flower. You see at night some flowers close their petals in order to protect their pollen from predators. It is in the presence of the sun that it opens and stretches. In the midst of your situation you need to reach out to the Son and take a deep breath.

Do you know who did a lot of crying in the bible? David. He would be considered a cry baby by today's standards. Read through the book of Psalms and you will see that even the Man after God's own heart shed some seriously needed tears. Pay close attention because all that crying he did was to God and each time he did God heard him and responded to him. Are you any less of a child of God than David was? Definitely not. Was David a perfect Christian? Uh no! What did David have that gave him the accolade of a man after God's own heart? Sometimes the deepest relationships are connected through tears.

There are three things that I learned about crying in the midst of my situation and I hope that they can help you as well.

1. Crying to the wrong person is a bad idea

2. Crying means something to God

3. Crying out can make you victorious

Crying to the wrong person is a bad idea!

Cry: A fit of weeping.

When upset, we tend to call up those good friends, that close family member or just someone that will listen to what we have to say. A lot of times we aren't even looking for any answers to our situation but that don't stop people from giving their two cents about what they think is best for our life. Most people when they give advice are just trying to help but when we take their advice and run with it is when we go wrong. How many times do you talk to someone and they have a personal agenda concerning your situation?

"Go cry unto the gods which ye have chosen; let them deliver you in the time of your tribulation."

Judges 10:14

As Janet Jackson so aptly put it "What have you done for me lately?" What does it mean to drive a Lamborghini when you are having panic attacks? What purpose does the money in your bank account serve when depression has you curled up in a ball in the middle of your bed? What is it that your family, friends or associates can do when you feel like the world is crashing around you? How can they fix your situation? It takes some of us more time to figure this out than others but there is little that friends or families can do to help unless they know how to get a prayer through to God. At this point some turn to alcohol, drugs or other things but still nothing helps. Now what do you do? You turn to the one that has answers to your questions. He can give you rest through the night when you should be tossing and turning. Not just any type of rest but the rest that makes you drool all over your pillow and snore real loud. God is the right one for you to cry out to.

Crying to the right person can be the difference between deliverance and suffering. In Matthew 9 there were two blind men who cried to Jesus. They didn't call their family, their friends or their neighbors but they called on Jesus and were healed. I know you must be thinking, "It can't really be that easy." I didn't think it could be that easy either but obviously these two blind knew the power in crying out to the right one. Not only did they cry out to Jesus but they bragged about what He had done after they were healed.

It's all about who you know. How many times has this remark been mentioned throughout every aspect of the media? Too many to count I'm sure. That's how you get the V.I.P. treatment wherever you go. Well as children of God we have V.I.P status as well and it grants us favor and mercy.

Jesus was curt: "You yourself said it. And that's not all. Soon you'll see it for yourself: The Son of Man seated at the right hand of the Mighty One, Arriving on the clouds of heaven."

Matthew 26:64 MSG

Jesus sits at the right hand of the Father to intercede on our behalf. If that isn't V.I.P. service then I don't know what is. Imagine going to a hotel and the right hand man of the owner takes any concerns or needs that you have right to the owner. Wow. Now that's power. We have the spiritual hook up.

Don't Stop Crying Out!

Outcry: an instance of crying; as an inarticulate utterance of distress, rage or pain.

When you cry out to God keep Him as your focus. What happened as a child when you really wanted something? You went to your parents, grandparents, aunts, uncles or whoever would listen and repeatedly brought what you desired to their attention. You didn't stop until you had someone on your side. Why don't we show that same enthusiasm when it comes to crying out to God? Sure, we curse Him for letting the situation happen and then we cry out to Him for help but what do we do after that? Do you continue to go to God until you get an answer? You should. Continue to cry out to God through prayer, fasting and reading His Word. Don't let go of the joy you want to receive.

Crying out is about healing, joy, pain or fear. The tears we shed are often more helpful than we think. They allow us to do something that society has emphasized as being weak. The tears we shed allow us to realize that we are human. We are not super heroes. Our tears are not like kryptonite to Superman, robbing us of our super powers, or salt on a slug, melting away our existence and killing us. They give us the ability to release things that can be mentally,

emotionally and spiritually harmful if we

hold on to them. What do you have bottled

up within your heart? Take a moment to

write them down on a piece of paper. Fold

up that paper and place it in your bible and I

will give you instructions on what to do with

it at the end of this chapter.

Crying Out on Behalf of Others

Cry: the public voice raised in protest or approval

What about when people cry out to us? Well, that's when you cry out to God on their behalf. A lot of times there are people in our lives that we wish we could hand them the world on a platter with all the trimmings but we can't. That's not saying that we love them any less or that their situation is not of importance to us. It's just that we can't be everything to everybody no matter how hard we try. For many reasons people will be drawn to you. Whether it's a stranger on public transportation, friends and

family, someone at your place of
employment or just someone in a store,
someone is always willing to strike up a
conversation. There is something about you
that makes people want to pour out their
heart to you.

"And the children of Israel said to Samuel,
Cease not to **cry** unto the LORD our God for us,
that he will save us out of the hand of the
Philistines."

I Samuel 7:8 KJV

People are drawn to your success.People
will notice how you come out of your
situation. Imagine it, the children of Israel

said Don't Stop Crying Out to God because that's how we will be saved. There will be people who are drawn to you because of your dependence on God. I often think of Jesus and the woman with the issue of blood in Matthew 9: 20-22, Mark 5:25-34 & Luke 8:43-47. That woman needed help. She had exhausted every resource she had but then she heard about Jesus and the things He had done. She knew He had a direct connection with God. He had to or else He wouldn't have been able to do the miracles she had heard about. The woman pushed through the crowd and touched Jesus' garment. Immediately she was healed. How many people do you think came to her to ask her

how she had gotten healed? Talk about
overnight celebrity status.

That's what happens as we are healed,
brought out, given strength and guided on
the right path by God. People want to know,
"How did you do it?" We are then given the
opportunity to give our testimony because
they are eager to find out what "remedy" we
used. How many people outside of church
know how good God has been to you? Do
you have that glow or are you walking
around angry and upset all the time? Are
you showing off the goodness of God?

People are drawn to what God has placed

inside you.As a child of God you have

become a light. What happens when you

shine a light into a dark room? The light cuts

through the darkness and you as a light of

Christ can cut through the darkness of other

people's situations with words of

encouragement, love and understanding.

That's why they are drawn to you. Just like

bugs to a light outside your home, people

will be attracted to what God has placed on

the inside of you. The things that every

person seeks in life makes us stand out in a

crowd. Peace, Love, Joy and the ability to

let go of what should be bothering us is

every persons' desire. When they see that

you have what they want they want to find

out how you got it. Have you ever had

someone befriend you and you have no idea

how the two of you became friends?

Crying means something to God

Cry: entreaty, appeal < a cry for help>

If God has numbered the hairs on our head why wouldn't he pay that much attention to what is causing us pain? Like any father he does not like to see us hurting but he will not step in until you ask him to. Think about the friends that you have. I'm not talking about a fair weather friend but a friend who you know inside and out. When they call you crying as a true friend you allow them to tell you what's going on without any interruption. (Interrupting them shows a lack of maturity because without knowing the whole story you can't give support) The connection you have with them respects that they are in pain. We only offer advice, criticism, or response after they ask for it. God is that type of friend to us.

"He has never let you down, never looked the other way when you were being kicked around. He has never wandered off to do His own thing; He has been right there listening."

Psalms 22:24 MSG

God listens to us. He listens to us because He cares about us. That is completely different from someone who just hears us. To me, that means that He hears our words but He also listens to their meaning. The same way that a parent knows that a child who doesn't want to go to school can mean that there is a bully they are trying avoid. The depth of our crying is often more than being hurt. Earlier I described three reasons why I cried when my daughter explained to me the details of the molestation.

1. My daughters' innocence was gone
2. I couldn't protect my little princesses
3. The effects of the offense would last longer than their childhood

God heard the underlining concerns through my crying. Not only did He hear them, He gave me His Word concerning them. What God heard while I cried was that I was scared for my daughters for three reasons. The first reason was the emotional and mental scars that I wouldn't be able to see with my eyes. Would they take this experience negatively into their adulthood creating a self-damaging image? Did they blame themselves for what happened? The second reason was the breach in their circle of protection. Will they have issues with trusting people? How would this affect their future friendships, marriages etc? The third reason was how this would affect our future as a family. Would they no longer have a relationship with their father, step mother, step sister and step brother? One way to see how far ahead God's plan for us reaches is to look back at all that He has already done.

Scars

Scars tell a story. As we all know, scars can last a lifetime. I personally still have scars from playing football with the neighborhood boys. (Yes, I was a tomboy) I also have a scar from falling off a fence at school. Those are the physical scars that most of us have come in contact with but we also have emotional scars. To this day, I still fight back tears when I think about the first time I was ever called a nigger. As a teenager in Philadelphia it caught me way off guard. I think it hurt it me more from shock because at the time I was one of a few African American youth that lived on our block. I'm talking about in 1996 way after slavery and equal rights. That emotional moment in my life could have made me bitter inside but instead I became curious about other cultures. How would you have reacted?

Look around you and I am sure your will see people with scars. You can see the scars in how they interact with other people, how they dress and even how they talk. Have you ever thought about what the 13 year girl wearing the tight clothes went through when she was 7 or 8? What about the 15 year boy who doesn't want to do any work in school?

Scars are a memory of what we have already made it through. They come from the wounds we obtain both willingly as a means to fit in or unwillingly as the result of someone else's actions.

"He heals the brokenhearted and binds up their wounds"
Psalms 147:3

God heals our wounds. Whew. That's a relief. So when a father or mother is missing in your life, God will heal you. When you've been abused, God will heal you. When depression has taken a toll on you, God will heal you. Repeat it to yourself over and over again. God will heal me. God has healed me. He has already given His Word and His Word is money in the bank. That means that my daughters have already been healed from the molestation because I took authority over it on their behalf. God healed them.

So now you're looking at the book wondering, "So what about the scars?" The scars are your blueprint to new beginnings. How so you ask. Remember that maze I described to you? Well let's go back to it. When you are going through a maze there will be times when you bump into a wall or you get scratched by a twig. Those are the times when we give in to temptation or we allow offense and anger to derail us from the path God has for us. Going through the maze is not always a walk around the block. It is, as Pastor Susan Smith would say, "A Process". What you went through that has you reading this book was a process. The individuals who came back to the church after backsliding went through a process. Scars are what you can have after you give a situation to God and allow Him to heal you.

Once God has healed you, you have to learn to let it go. I say it because everyone's "it" may be different but they all serve the same purpose as an obstacle in our life. Once you get healed you can't go back and try to peel off the scab. The scab is there to help in the healing process. Beneath the scab new skin cells are being made to repair the torn skin and damaged blood vessels are being fixed. (kidshealth.org) God is fixing and repairing some things in your life during times when you feel uncomfortable or stretched. That can mean that if you've been removed from the presence of certain individuals, situations or places then that is your scab. For me, the move from Pennsylvania to Maryland was necessary in my healing process but it felt as nasty to me as a physical scab. No one likes to have no choices when it comes to moving their family. I had no idea what God was doing or why He couldn't do it closer to the majority of my family. The thing I learned was that God knows how to heal the seen and unseen wounds in our life leaving us with scars to understand what we have made it through.

Protection

We find security in our Father's arms.
I'm so grateful that God's means of
protection are so much more dependable
than the world's. Can we be real about this?
How is the world protecting your children?
Drugs are not just on the corner anymore.
The drugs have been brought into the school
where our children should be learning. How
is the world protecting your finances?
Scandals are coming to the light and big
name companies are closing. How is the
world protecting you? Do you have
bodyguards? I didn't get one. God's means
of protection are clear and simple.

Protection in my eyes is not just saving me when I know I need help but also safeguarding me from the dangers I may not see. Dictionary.com defines protection as:

1. Act of defending, guarding, or preserving or the state of being so protected
2. Thing, person, or group that defends or guards
3. Patronage
4. Guarantee against risk

God's definition of protection is:

"Because he set his love on Me, therefore I will save him; I will set him [securely] on high, because he knows My name [he confidently trusts and relies on Me, knowing I will never abandon him, no, never].

Psalms 91:14 AMP

So let me get this right. I have protection and I'm able to be delivered just because I know my Saviors name and love Him? Yes. Yes. Yes. What does the protection of God mean in my everyday life? Those we love we have a relationship with and there is constant communication. Think about it. The family members that you are close to you make a habit to call and check up on them regularly. How is your communication with God? Are you only ringing Heaven's phone when you need something or are you in CONSTANT communication with Him?

Seasoned saints have been taught this at sometime in your life. If this is new to you or even if it's something you've heard before than start with 15 minutes reading a scripture and praying. A relationship with God is the relationship of a father and a child. He desires to protect those close to His heart.

Often any reference to relationships with fathers gets easily pushed aside or buried. Today, there are many young men & young women growing up without a father in the home. That presence is being replaced by single mothers, mentors and male family members but that doesn't weaken the power of fatherhood. A father can and will provide the framework for children moving into adulthood emotionally, spiritually, mentally and physically. That father does not have to be a biological father but they will provide the same key elements to maturity. This is a scar for me as well as many other men, women and children. I will discuss this more in a later chapter but I found that even as an adult I needed a mentor/father figure in order to move forward in my life. It helped me to grow in my personal life as well as my spiritual life.

"for the Lord reproves him who he loves, as a father the son in whom he delights."

Proverbs 3:12

Let's briefly discuss the "Love" part of our protection plan. The things and people we hold dear are usually the things and people we fight for. Don't act like you haven't ever run to the rescue of something you felt was important to you. I can remember having a huge argument with a close friend after he spilled a beverage on my son's car. Not just any car. One of those expensive motorized cars that my son could ride in. Yes the argument was heated and my mother had to step in the middle of us before it got physical. Now when I think about it, and I'm sure as you are reading this paragraph, I realize that it was just a car. My son loved that car at that time but if I ask him now he probably doesn't even remember having the car. Now let's think about how this relates to our relationship with God. God loves us even more than my son loved that car. His son died for our soul just like I was ready to fight for that car. So why wouldn't He want to protect what His son died for? We have the ultimate protection plan when we learn to cry out to God.

"God is the bedrock under my feet, the castle in

which I live, my rescuing knight. My God the high crag where I run for dear life, hiding behind the boulders, safe in the granite hideout."
Psalm 18:2 MSG

When we are in the midst of a situation we never think to be thankful. Why? The situation could have been a lot worse. They were covered under God's protection plan because even when I wasn't praying for my children, someone was. Think about your own situation. You were covered under God's protection plan because there was someone praying for you. We now have the opportunity to have a personal protection plan with God. Insurance policies have a payment plan in order for you to continue to be covered. When you stop the payments your coverage ends. God's protection plan is no different. It starts when you cry out to God and it only stops when we stop communicating with God. As simple as this may sound it is a process to change our mindset. It may be hard but it is not impossible.

God's protection doesn't save us from our decisions. Look at the life of David. When he was in direct communication with God he was protected, strong and stood out from ordinary men because he was doing the will of God. Once he chose to abandon his dependence on God he suffered greatly. There are those who argue that when the child of David and Bathsheba died it was because God was getting revenge for what David did but that's not the case. God's protection is directly related to our relationship with him. David, before this moment had a constant communication with God yet when he saw Bathsheba in 2 Samuel 11 he didn't talk to God about it. He chose to go to bed with a married woman and didn't talk to God about it. He chose to deceive a man who willingly fought for him and didn't talk to God about it. How would that whole situation have been different if David had chosen to speak to God and acted on what God told him to do instead of his own instincts? God's didn't stop protecting David. David walked away from God's protection.

"All your life, no one will be able to hold out against you. In the same way I was with Moses, I'll be with you. I won't give up on you; I won't leave you."
Joshua 1:5 MSG

"Don't panic/ I'm with you. There's no need to fear for I'm your God. I'll give you strength. I'll help you. I'll hold you steady, keep a firm grip on you."
Isaiah 41:10 MSG

The promises God has given to us He will not deny us. God's protection can already be seen in your life. Take a moment to think about what God has brought you through. How has your relationship with God not only changed your surroundings but kept you from harm? God protects what and who is precious to Him just like we protect what and who is important to us. You are a flower that is about to blossom. He killed the weeds in your life and He pruned anything that could hold you back from growing. That is included in His protection plan.

Future

My today is not my forever. Now on to the future! We save for our future. We plan for our future. We pay out money for the best education for our children's future. Then what happens? We lose focus when something comes up that we didn't plan for or we get stressed out when things don't go according to plan. All that planning we did just to get to a fork in the road and sit down. I am in no way saying that planning is a bad thing. It's just that there is a difference between our master plan and the Master's plan.

"For I know the plans I have for you, the Lord,

plans for welfare and not for evil, to give you a

future and a hope."

Jeremiah 29:11

How much less would you stress about the

questions of your future if you knew it was

already planned out? Even better how about

if you knew the situation you were going

through was leading you into your next

phase in a much bigger plan? Hmmm.

Sounds good right? Well, that is just what

Jeremiah 29:11 is telling us. God has a plan

for ever situation that happens in your life

and it's a plan that is good. Don't believe

me?

"The thief comes only to steal and kill and destroy. I came that they may have life and have it abundantly."

John 10:10

The abundant life is about more than things. The abundant life is about enjoying life to the fullest everyday. Not only does God have good plans for us but Christ came to give us the abundant life.

Did you make a list of situations and people who have hurt you in some way from earlier in the book? Well pull out that list, look at it and say "My destiny is too great for me to be upset about what you did in my past. I forgive you and I am moving on." Then take

the paper, or papers, and rip it to shreds.
After you've taken out some stress on the
pieces of paper throw them in the trash and
leave them there. You may shed some tears
and that's okay. Think of this as the process
of shedding old skin in order to move
forward.

In order to have the abundant life you have
to be able to declare that God is in control of
your life and not people, things or situations.
The enemy will use past pains to keep us
inactive in our walk with God. Those are the
times when we begin to feel we are
unworthy of God's love and therefore we
don't seek out the promises He has given us.

It's time to break loose from the strongholds and walk in divine favor. Your future is great, even with the obstacles and detours, because that is how God designed it.

Crying out can make you victorious

Cry: proclamation

Crying Out is not just about tears, its words! What does it mean when we proclaim and decree things in our life? It means that we are speaking present and future portions of our life. The words we speak are blueprints to our destiny because the words we speak come from our heart. Your heart and mouth are good girlfriends sharing gossip with each other or guy friends in high school sharing second base stories. God shows us throughout His Word that the two are closely connected and when you change what's in your heart you change what comes out your mouth as well.

"O generation of vipers, how can ye, being evil, speak good things? For out of the abundance of the heart the mouth speaketh."
Matthew 12:34

"Keep thy heart with all diligence; for out of it are the issues of life."
Proverbs 4:23

There are things that we seem to have the hardest time keeping under control that get us in the most trouble. Our ears, eyes, heart and mouth can do some damage in our life more than anyone we come in contact with in our life. Did you notice that I put the mouth last in the list? Once we have said things out our mouth there is no way to take it back. I didn't put our mind on the list because it reciprocates what we put in it while the organs I mentioned have the ability to alter things. When we see and hear things we have the option to hold onto it, let it go or alter our perception of it. Holding onto things gives that person, thing or situation a place in our heart. My pastor always says, "The heart is the birth place of our increase." Well if we are not careful it can be the birth place of decrease.

Decreeing and declaring comes from what's in your heart. Okay so how do we get things in our heart? Reading the Word, listening to messages and going over our notes from service give us the opportunity to chew our spiritual food. The more you listen to something the more it sticks. For example, have you ever heard a song over and over again on the radio? What happened next? You would be humming the tune and singing the words because the melody was stuck in your head. Let's take it even deeper. What happens to the child who is told over and over again that they will never be anything? It becomes ingrained in their mind and they start to believe what they are told. Repetition is a very powerful tool that can either build someone up or break someone to pieces..

"Death and life are in the power of the tongue: and they that love it shall eat the fruit thereof." Proverbs 18:21

We can learn a lot from David's mouth. He spoke some good things into his life when he was walking in the steps God ordered for him but he also spoke some painful situations into his life when he was in the flesh. He spoke someone else's wife into his bed and reaped the death of his child. How many times have we spoken ill will to the things we were impregnated with? Saying, I give up or I will never be able to do something is just as damaging as what David did. Yet when David was in the midst of battle, before his battles and after his battles he cried out to God. It's when we don't seek God that we damage the path to our destiny and then we have to take a detour. Let's see what happens when we seek God.

Before

It's time for a plan. Have you ever noticed that when you plan things out it goes a whole lot smoother? Planning a graduation party seems less of a hassle than just having people come over and figuring it out as you go. Preparation sets the pace for the journey ahead. Pastor Ray Smith says, "It is better to prepare than to repair." So how do you prepare for life? I asked that same question. We can't prepare for the circumstances that occur in life specifically because we don't know when, where or what will happen. We can prepare for life when we choose to cry out to God before we make decisions as situations occur or in the midst of our situations.

"When I cry unto thee, then shall mine enemies turn back: this I know; for God is for me."

Psalms 56:9

Let's take a ride down memory lane. How many times have you been prepared to fight someone and then quit when you saw they had a group of people standing with them? Maybe it was the other way around and people went running scared when you walked up with your posse. Why did they run away from the fight? They were scared plain and simple. In Psalms 56:9, David said when, not if, he cried out to God his enemies turned back. Just like the scenario in Junior High, they ran away because they were scared of who David had with him. We can take it a step further by saying that his enemies were scared because of who David knew since his enemies did not see a physical presence. So who you know can make a difference.

Before the situation happened with my daughters my prayer life consisted of saying grace over my food and saying prayers at bedtime. I knew that it was important to speak to God but I never thought it was a necessity. I felt that saying prayer before bed pretty much covered me for the next day. Besides, I was busy with three children, work, cooking and cleaning. Does this sound familiar? I was confusing quantity with quality. Does how much time we spend praying really matter? No, it's not about how much time we spend praying that matters. What matters is how we talk to God, when we talk to God and what are we talking to God about.

We have to remember that God is our Bridegroom. When you wake up in the morning do you say good morning to your parents, children, husband or wife? Do you tell them about your day or call to just say hi? Do you only talk to the people who are important in your life when you have a problem? God patiently waits for us to tell him about our day, say good morning, give thanks and not just tell him about what we need or what is going wrong. That desire can be seen all throughout His Word in the experience of others. Take some time to talk to God and read His Word to see what He has to say about your situation.

This can be applied to our everyday walk with God. We can prepare our spirit by being refilled and renewed through prayer. Prayer can be like a fresh oil change for our spirit. When we don't talk to God on a regular basis the enemy uses this gap in our prayer life as a foothold. During this time is when small things begin to agitate us and get us off track in our spiritual walk. Like the paper that someone jammed in the printer and left it like that or the rush hour traffic that is making you late for a meeting. When we pray in the morning, it doesn't stop these things from happening but it does put us in a different mindset allowing us to deal with the situation in a rational manner.

"Now in the morning, having risen a long while before daylight, He went out and departed to a solitary place; and there he prayed."

Mark 1:35

Jesus, knowing the journey He had ahead of Him, woke up early to speak to God before starting His day. Take a moment to think about how powerful that statement is. Jesus, the son of God, started His day by talking to the Father. Most of us try to fit talking to God into our schedule instead of fitting our schedule around talking to God. He is not a peg to a light bright that you can use anywhere. He is a puzzle piece. Without him our life is incomplete and He has a special place where only He can fit. When we miss breakfast in the morning it affects our whole day. We become sluggish. We can't focus. Our stomach starts growling during a business meeting. Without being spiritually fed in the morning we get the same results.

It's a matter of confidence in who is on your side that makes us unafraid of what may come our way. So what does that mean in the everyday? Stop, talk to God and then shut your mouth and listen to the instructions God gives. This is how we prepare for our day that will be filled with the enemy's attempts to derail us from our heavenly mission. Our most important goal is about saving souls and what better way to show someone the love of God is there than living it?

"The fruit of the righteous is a tree of life; and he that winneth souls is wise."

Proverbs 11:30

During

What do you do in the "in between" times? In the midst of your situation do you curse God or do you call out to God? So many times we curse God for what's happening in our life instead of asking Him why it is happening, what you need to learn from it or even asking him to give you the strength to endure. I know. It's so much easier to throw in the towel when things get rough. Remember we discussed that God has a plan for us and that doesn't change when we get into a situation.

"You were forged a strong scepter by God of Zion; now rule, though surrounded by enemies."
Psalms 110:2 MSG

"When I walk into the thick of trouble, keep me alive in the angry turmoil. With one hand strike my foes, with your other hand save me."
Psalm 138:7 MSG

Don't give up. It may look like the odds are against you but you have someone beside you that is more powerful than any situation. He has the power to save us and defeat our enemies at the same time. God have given us the promise that He will protect us and that doesn't change when we have given in

to temptation or fallen behind in our bible
readings. Instead of looking around for help
look up and call out to God.

What you are going through will not last
forever. In the midst of a situation it always
takes on the illusion that it will never end.
Sister, brother, friend, family or associate I
want you to say this out loud with authority.
"This is not my forever! This is only my
today!" Now, don't just say it. Live it. Don't
allow what happened today to affect your
tomorrow. Don't allow it to affect your next
hour. When we allow a situation to take root
in our heart it replays over and over again
stealing our joy. If we take authority when a

situation happens we start the process of moving forward in our lives.

Shut the devil up. No I'm not substituting curse words. During a situation the enemy will try to keep you upset and sad. He will do all he can to make you feel like no one understands your situation or that people won't believe you. The list of tactics he uses could probably cover the globe but you have the authority to shut him down. Get aggressive and speak happiness over your life, speak joy over your life, speak peace over your life and tell the enemy that you already have the victory.

"No test of temptation that comes your way is beyond the course of what others have had to face. All you need to remember is that God will never let you down; he'll never let you be pushed past your limit; he'll always be there to help you come through it."
1 Corinthians 10:13 MSG

You are not alone. Yes, I know that this is a song title but I also want you to understand that this is encouragement. We often get to the point in any situation where we feel alone. That is the point when we curse ourselves for any decisions we made that brought us to this moment. God hasn't left your side. Even though you may feel that you can't move forward I beseech you to take a few more steps. The end is closer than you think and as things become a heavy burden turn and give them to God.

Don't walk away from your blessing. In Luke 23, Jesus was nailed to the cross with a thief on a cross on either side of Him. One chose to mock Jesus along with the guards while the other said "Jesus, remember me when you enter your kingdom." (Luke 23:42 MSG) We are blessed to have Jesus sitting on the right hand of the Father to speak on our behalf. That means that when you have the opportunity to pray in Jesus name there is change waiting to happen.

After

It's time to party!!!!!! Victory is yours and the enemy has retreated or been defeated. This is the time that we can see the knowledge we have learned along the way. Don't be afraid to give God some praise because the "what if" possibilities are endless and the enemy will use those "what if" possibilities to block us from moving forward. The "what if" possibilities are the things your mind wanders to when we think about what did happen in comparison to what could have happened. That's the time to dance, sing, write, paint or do cartwheels to get your praise on.

"I sing to God, the Praise-Lofty, and find myself safe and saved."

Psalm 18:3 MSG

Look towards the future and leave the past behind. Don't be like Lot's wife in Genesis 19, God delivered her and her husband from death's grip but she turned around to look at what they were leaving behind. How many times do we get caught up in situations we had already been delivered from because we thought we were missing out on something? How many times have we run back to someone who continues to hurt us because we felt that we deserve to have what we want? Don't look back at what you had because God's got something better in store for you.

"And it came to pass, when they brought out those kings unto Joshua, that Joshua called for all the men of Israel, and said unto the captains of the men of war which went with him, Come near, put your feet upon the necks of these kings. And they came near, and put their feet upon the necks of them." Joshua 10:24 KJV

This is your moment to put your situation under your feet. Tread upon what once had control over your life. Take your authority back and show the enemy that you are still moving towards your destiny. Whatever obstacle he put in your way simply made you take a detour on your journey. You can stomp, shout or take a victory lap around your home. Just don't break anything.

Truthfully, I use to think that people who shouted were crazy. All that jumping and stomping was too much in my eyes until God showed it to me through His eyes. Someone shouting is sick and tired of the enemy. They are stomping on every negative situation that has been brought their way and shouting praises unto God. Most of these people shout in their vehicle, during service, at home or in their prayer closet. I don't want you to be misled. Not everyone flipping down the isle is Holy Ghost filled but those who are definitely have a testimony or a message to share. God is doing something in their life so move to the side and let them go.

"Abner then said, "I'm ready. Let me go now to rally everyone in Israel for my master, the king. They'll make a treaty with you, authorizing you to rule them however you see fit." Abner was sent off with David's blessing."

2 Samuel 3:21 MSG

A war is never finished without setting up a treaty. That contract states what is going to change, what can stay the same and what the future will hold if the treaty is not kept. God had a treaty written out for each situation we encounter. The Bible will show you exactly what needs to change in your life, what can stay the same and what will happen if the treaty isn't kept. I encourage you to look up a situation similar to what you went through in the Bible and study it. God will show you your treaty with Him. Our treaty with God started the moment you accepted Christ as your personal Savior.

Your treaty is also your security. In the

world, a treaty gives you the protection from the country or person your treaty is with but it's dependant upon who is the decision maker at the time. Our treaty with God will never change unless we change it. We have the ability to decide how much trust we put in our treaty with God. When we put our faith in God He responds to our level our faith.

After your situation did you trust God more or did your trust Him less? I trusted Him more after reading what God had done for all the mothers in the Bible. What God does for one won't He do for us? I gave more and more to Him when I realized that He could do more with my situation than I could. My faith in God was all I had.

My victory didn't feel like a victory at the moment. After being off from work for two months I was about to be homeless. I had no idea what I was going to do but when I handed my situation over to God He showed up and showed out. We moved in with a family member which ended up being such a blessing to us. My children adjusted quickly and I enjoy seeing the smile on their faces each day. What the enemy meant for bad my God used for good. My children and I have bonded and they know that no matter what the situation may be that they can talk to me.

Love Shines Through

Love is gonna shine through

Above those who

Are gonna hate

Learn to appreciate

The love shining through the ceiling

You'll get the feeling

Sooner or later

That sweet type of flavor

© 2015

With all of my love,

Alliya D. Marshall

Scripture References

"Casting all your cares upon him, for he careth for you." I Peter 5:7

It's Okay to Cry!

"....weeping may endure for a night, but joy cometh in the morning."

Psalm 30:5

Crying out can make you victorious

"O generation of vipers, how can ye, being evil, speak good things? For out of the abundance of the heart the mouth speaketh."

Matthew 12:34

"Because he set his love on Me, therefore I will save him; I will set him [securely] on high, because he knows My name [he confidently trusts and relies on Me, knowing I will never abandon him, no, never].

Psalms 91:14 Amp

Above all else, guard your heart, for everything you do flows from it.

Proverbs 4:23 NIV

"Death and life are in the power of the tongue: and they that love it shall eat the fruit thereof."

Proverbs 18:21

Before

"When I cry unto thee, then shall mine enemies turn back: this I know; for God is for me."

Psalms 56:9

"Now in the morning, having risen a long while before daylight, He went out and departed to a solitary place; and there he prayed."

Mark 1:35

"The fruit of the righteous is a tree of life; and he that winneth souls is wise."
Proverbs 11:30

During

"You were forged a strong scepter by God of Zion; now rule, though surrounded by enemies."
Psalms 110:2 MSG

"When I walk into the thick of trouble, keep me alive in the angry turmoil. With one hand strike my foes, with your other hand save me."

Psalm 138:7 MSG

"No test of temptation that comes your way
is beyond the course of what others have had
to face. All you need to remember is that
God will never let you down; he'll never let
you be pushed past your limit; he'll always
be there to help you come through it."

1 Corinthians 10:13 MSG

After

"I sing to God, the Praise-Lofty, and find myself
safe and saved."

Psalm 18:3 MSG

"And it came to pass, when they brought out

those kings unto Joshua, that Joshua called

for all the men of Israel, and said unto the

captains of the men of war which went with

him, Come near, put your feet upon the

necks of these kings. And they came near,

and put their feet upon the necks of them."

Joshua 10:24 KJV

"Abner then said, "I'm ready. Let me go now

to rally everyone in Israel for my master, the

king. They'll make a treaty with you,

authorizing you to rule them however you

see fit." Abner was sent off with David's

blessing."

2 Samuel 3:21 MSG

Meet the Author

Altovise Pelzer, the author of "The PRESS", a series of self-help books for businesses, women and families, is the CEO of AP Business Consultants. Born and raised in Philadelphia, PA, Altovise was encouraged to write at the age of eight by her grandmother and she later found that developing a love of writing would get her through many difficult situations. What she didn't know, was that writing would also be a catalyst for her business, a gateway to connecting with youth and an opportunity to advocate for those who feel as though they have lost their voice.

Altovise is currently strengthening her passion of motivating women and youth through speaking, her holiday anti bullying youth initiative #GiftsForChange and in the pages of her first book series titled "The Press:Eight Stages of Pressing through difficult situations" She finds inspiration for her book series and conference topics from life experiences surrounding the molestation of her two daughters, fighting homelessness, the loss of her mother, learning to trust again and love. She encourages both women and youth to #KeepPRESSing no matter what circumstances they may find themselves in.

Altovise is a mother, sister, mentor, friend, motivational coach and advocate. With so many hats, Altovise finds joy in spending time with her children and siblings doing what she loves most which is simply laughing.

Ordering Information
Quantity Sales – Special discounts are available on quantity purchases by corporations, associations and others. For more details please contact the publisher at the email below.

contacts@altovisepelzer.com

Made in the USA
Columbia, SC
03 May 2022